were the *bees*

were the *bees*

ANDY WEAVER

Library and Archives Canada Cataloguing in Publication
Weaver, Andy, 1971–
Were the bees / Andy Weaver.

Poems.
ISBN 1-896300-85-5

I. Title.
PS8595.E175W47 2005   C811'.6   C2004-906666-8

Editor for the Press: Douglas Barbour
Cover image: From Thomas Moffett's book *Insectorum sive
minimorum animalium theatrum*, 1634.
Cover and interior design: Ruth Linka
Author photo: Kelly Laycock

NeWest Press acknowledges the support of the Canada Council for the Arts, the
Alberta Foundation for the Arts, and the Edmonton Arts Council for our publishing program.
We also acknowledge the financial support of the Government of Canada through the Book
Publishing Industry Development Program (BPIDP) for our publishing activities.

NeWest Press
201–8540–109 Street
Edmonton, Alberta
T6G 1E6
(780) 432-9427
www.newestpress.com

1   2   3   4   5   08   07   06   05

PRINTED AND BOUND IN CANADA

for my parents, Charlene and Everett,
who have always supported me—even when they didn't understand me.

Contents

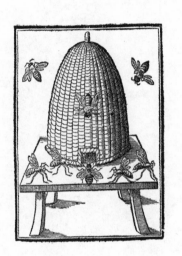

One

Sugar bleeds blue

                    -desire in its bowl
            drags on the air
                        like a long cigarette

            the fridgedoor is open
                    and breathing deep

            my ice cream is
        gaspingmeltingjoy

                    the plants
            are panting
                        blood
        hounds on a chase

    everything is electric
            religion of breath

                and then
            the last
        feathers
            of her perfume
        drift from the room

March 31, 2002

1

the sex in the morning is great
for me okay
for you

it's my 31st birthday

2

that afternoon my mother calls
to tell me her father
is dying of brain
tumours and has been for some
time without her
being told

she speaks the words to me
from three thousand miles away but
i hear them

my grandfather lives
2000 miles further away i
don't call him

between three
and five thousand miles
is the physical limit of grief

religions were built
with less proof than this

3

i am wearing your t-shirt
your ex-boyfriend gave you
with a lorca poem
written in spanish
on the front

the words feel unspeakably sad

you are asleep
in what will soon be
our bed

i don't know
what all this means i don't
even know
spanish

Five Letters to Venus, Standing Cold on her Shell

1.

On a bridge this evening, I watched the ospreys dive
into the river. Fall is coming, and, like Berryman before me, I'm
obsessed with thoughts of flying to the truest, deepest south.
But even this suffers from the terrible cliché—I just flew in from
despair, and my old, useless arms are tired.

2.

Course, there's really no reason, Madame Love, you should
help a poor cowpoke like me, we both know the horrible names I've
called you. In my defence, ma'am, I can only say my worst com-
plaints were always against Lust, that double-jointed little tart you
call sister. And now it seems Hope Springs, that crooked casino
where only the most desperate gamblers play, is the only game
around. I can hear the sheriff coming, and baby, he doesn't think his
town is big enough . . . Hell, you've heard that one a hundred times.
Lady Luck, you just roll them bones.

3.

For a second, I'll drop the mask, because I know you're a
nice lady, deep down. We've both read Wallace Stevens. I'm not
asking if there's a 14th way of looking at a blackbird, or what kind of
mind winter has. I need something so very, very simple. Put down
that blue guitar, stop your warbling, and tell me exactly how things
are. Or must I, too, die after placing honey on the altar?

4.

　　　Nobody says you have to get off that clam-shell, put on a business suit and get a job. All we'd like to know is: do you really know what you're doing? Why do you keep rubbing the cat the wrong way?

5.

　　　There's a wisp of amnesia in every successful affair, that's all I've learned. The way I stumbled to her bed each time for the first time. Our bodies like a long-lost treatise on the stars, all the pages dog-eared in my mind. All I've learned is there's a wisp of amnesia in every successful affair. Love, I would like you to help me forget her.

Judas, before

I fell asleep, praying in the garden.

In a dream, my mind was filled with visions of timepieces
tattooed on my arms. My skin uncoiled
and the precision of my body could be seen.
My heart kept its own time.

In another, the sky was clear and I stared at the stars whirling
above me. The wind swam madly between them.
My blood moved quietly. Dark birds
had flocked to my house.

When I woke, a worm had slipped round
my finger, a cold, black ring.
Shadows of trees swayed over my body.

There are things harder than stones
to get answers from.

My face, as seen in the glass that covers a print of
Modigliani's 1918 portrait of Jeanne Hébuterne

I.
To know just once
that you've got it right,
boil it down to its base elements
and chart it all, x and y,
topographical and precise.

Lately I've been obsessed
with reflections, their breezy trickery.
It's easy to spot the carnival distortions,
when you're thirty feet
tall and 600 pounds,
but they have so many other games,
the slight puffing or curving of cheeks,
the light sometimes catching the bald spot,
how a mouth is never quite
the same two days in a row.
Or now, my right eye embedded
in this woman's belly, my left
held softly in her hand.
There's something here, something
almost flittering through.

I would like to close my eyes
and walk away, leave my face
in this glass.

II.
Her face is
calm,
there's no other
word for it. A metaphor
would only be arrogant.

Dim, a ghost, my face
is slippage, transitory, and it seems
that her head has assumed
the angle of pity.
Next to hers, my face is March,
neither lion nor lamb,
a face caught in the change
of its seasons: the days are warm
but there are no leaves on the trees,
my shoes are always muddy,
and I'm always dressed
too lightly for the night-chill.

III.
At times this face has a strength,
under certain . . . weak lights.
But let's stay away
from the fairy tales and suffer
through a little truth: it has the strength
of the weak and the strength
only to stay weak, the way
a wounded bird, flittering
madly on the grass,
reaches madly at an open sky.

IV.
Luckily, I've decided
to believe this face
is a cliché, a lie
that can be played
for comedy: *Have you heard*
the one about
the pig-faced poet?
He spent his life
trying to rewrite Hamlet.

Shaving in the mirror, I tell myself
this means that tragedy
is always
only a way station.

Tangle

Nicola, who would have thought
you'd be walking days after breaking
your pelvis, or dancing in a bar weeks later
while Tim and I slam-danced away
the Old Year like a blister that needed
to be lanced.

But you've always carried surprise
like wine in a sack on your hip—
your story of a broken nose in India,
a drugged watermelon in Turkey.
Or the time I opened your front door,
hungover from beer, from crashing
on your couch,
wearing only jeans and a frown,
and stared confusedly into the chests
of two huge, huge Mounties.
I couldn't remember your last name
when they asked who lived there.
(Later, we laughed at the cops, the way
they went away smiling, thinking *that Nicola*
must be quite an easy
girl with the guys.)

Or your flashes of anger, so
rare and awful, like the time
everyone stared from the truck

while you argued at
Tim on the street corner,
4:30 in the morning,
all of us forgetting
to envy him.

There's an Egyptian poem
taped to my bedroom wall:
Death is before me today
like the odour of myrrh.
But who has time to stop
and smell the myrrh
in this day and age?

Death is before me today
like a man's home-coming after the wars abroad.
But death is less before me today
than a poem taped to my wall.

Of course I've thought about it,
in passing, even flirted with it a few times
in a fumbling, try-to-strike-up-a-conversation-
with-the-woman-in-front-of-me-
in-the-grocery-check-out-line kind of way.
I imagine death is bland,

that it must taste like everything
else, just like chicken, so they say.
Ignorance: I'm a vegetarian.
But I'm nervous now
and making bad jokes at death's expense.

The fact of the matter is
I've never been to a funeral.
I've never had anyone
die on me, never even
had an old pet move
to Aunt Sally's farm.

Nic, who would have thought
that you would almost be the first,
stepping carelessly in front of a car?
I didn't, I didn't
expect Tim's phone call saying
no brain damage, I didn't
even think of brain damage before that,
I didn't expect your bruised face or blood
-red eye either. This is
a poem of ignorance
as much as it is a poem
of skin grafts, of pins
put into your arm.   .

The hospital room smells
funny (the faint odour of myrrh?),
all of us huddled in
and returning day after day
with our sad presents and silly smiles,
the flowers taking over the room.
Tim does his bit,
eating your food
while he's feeding you,
and you offer us a smile
like a finely-grown garden.
And I think it's then
that I realize we are all,
secretly, madly
in love with you and,
through you,
with each other.
For days you are like our only
fresh water, the only wall
against the winter wind,
and you somehow never look
too small for the job.

The room becomes thick
with life, thick with our lives,
like the flowers blooming in the corner,
and we all tangle beautifully.
No one expected this.

destination

1. departure

moving like a soundwave,
you're aimless dissipation,

rosethorn-fire
in the fingertips.

you led me
into a dark alley.

2. journey

moving,

like a sound-thorn,
aimless wave
dissipation.

you arose,
led your darkly all
into me,

fingertips in
the fire.

3. destination

move.
wave your aimless
ing like a dark,
lead, alley-sound.

thorn-fire eros
in the finger
tips
me into you.

dissipation.

blood lust

like the blood that circles
monthly the drain of her shower
there's a certain song
my lady plays
when I am her instrument

somehow natural and
somehow unholy

like a predator
of the butterfly

odin plucked out his eye for sight
drank wise kvasir's blood for song

two spots on the bedsheet
a scrape on my arm
and your period

are the bridges stronger
for this spilling of iron

so much of you trickling
to the ground

when will the dazed earth
start looking for answers

the red lines in her
green eyes
                    a place
of meeting
foxes in the summer hillside

like whalesong
their simplest conversations
taking the level
of artistry

that night
on our backs
next to lake ontario

our blood finding
its own level
                    not
wishing on the shooting stars not
needing to

inside my ears
my lipsmy legs
my bloodrush
to pool in
you

this afternoon your blood
on the mouth
of the condom almost
too much
to throw away

To   [
in love with love and lousy poetry
                          The Weakerthans
][
Love—with, and, under, over,
through, around, in, out, in,
out, in, out—love:
poetry this lousy
to phoenixmend your
whens and ifs,
always eternitymixed
with who
][
united?
][
love, lousy love, (and in poetry!)
left with only the gist you got. so dream re
member: bass line hooked you
in the ass for once whiteboy you
grooved   you
millerground her robinhoodflour
she yeasted your dough you
enjoyed delicious rolls
][
untied.
][
and lousy   *in* love *with*   (¿poetry love?)
the night sending refracted
redshift desire out
ah   then   when   if
]to you   always
from you   all ways
from me   lousy
with love

[

21

C.

[or how i learned to write love poetry from page 147
of the New Webster's Dictionary]

*carbon, (kárbən) n. a tetravalent element (symbol C, at. no. 6, at. mass
12.01115). It occurs in crystalline forms as diamonds and graphite.
Combined with other elements, it occurs in all living things.*

her body, carbonaceous
riversilting softness,
lampblack hair flow
without diamond pointlessness
of matrix bright.
residual radioactive, she turns away
from animal respiration,
welds combustion tight
into this most aqueous container.
playing her catalytic role
she aerates this old Carbonari,
my heart, a saturation into acid
radical being, a process
held to be the source of energy
for the sun and for many stars.

Retraction (Turn up the Sad Songs)

Threatened with physical violence,
I'll gladly admit that your voice doesn't
hover in a room as a lace-like stream of smoke.
Men don't drift away comparing the wiggle
in your walk to smouldering
incense suspended thickly in the air.

Sure, I could tell you that on my guitar
you were always the G-string, pure
allure and appeal; but that's an instrument
I've never learned to play. And Lord knows
there's none of the violin in either of us, no
rich, velvety sorrow to root out and heal.
Even the tambourine, to be honest, seems too
exotic and complex for whatever we had.

Listen carefully; I was wrong: your breath
hasn't coated the inside of your house
with a thick, yellow honey, and bees, quite simply,
don't get confused and follow you home.
                                    True, there are
dark,
        focal
                moles on your back,
but it seems unlikely now that I ever
                really
mistook them for little islands
where my mouth hovered like rain
ready to break. And, even if I could,
I wouldn't fold my lips into your body
like petals damp with desire's dark scent
—you see, the few flowers we have left

to offer each other are stunted now
and warped like northern trees.

It feels odd to finally say this. I've been
the proverbial ostrich up to his neck in sand, and
maybe my excuse is that blood was gathered
in a place far from my head.
                            But,
                                    yes, you're right,
years from now I will still dream of your hair, brown
like polished oak, and the feel of my hand
on your belly. I may even, in the daze of waking,
check to see if your navel left a mark on my palm.
It's a strange, lasting thing, when a fool for love turns
out to be just a fool.

Sparrows

1.

Springs in the world's great clock,
pips behind the song's soloist, delicate
initiates of the wind, who will ever conquer
the small alps of your spines? How can we
know your theories on gravity's dark
exchange, or put into practice your studies
on Brownian Movement? Little dictationists,
what secret don't you know?

2.

Catullus said that if you put a poem
in a drawer and like it five years later, then
it's worth sharing. No sparrow could survive
a test of art this mundane. Perspective is not
always the keystone to wisdom.

3.

Advent calendar on the fridge
of a friend I'd assumed was as irreligious as I,
the wings of a sparrow folded to its body
always strike me as a small yet remarkable act
of grace, the best evidence the world
has offered me of the existence of God.

4.

Once, on a lonely walk down
my street under a dark winter sky, you burst
from a hedge, a soft reminder that
the moon is every bit as there on nights
it is new as when it is full. How
many times had you been there before?

5.

I offer this as apology for my
arrogance: smallest darts from a larger hand,
rejoicers in the tiniest of seeds, vigilant choirs
of combined movement, always know you
are proof we live in a loved world.

Kandinsky's Composition VIII
(for four simultaneous voices)

We must keep in mind that language [in atomic physics] can only be used as it is used in poetry where it is not its purpose to precisely describe given facts but rather to create images and inspire thoughts in the mind of the listener.

Niels Bohr, quoted in *Kandinsky*

1.	2.	3.	4.
paths cut			
with no thought			
of followers	river		
	feels the first		
liquid as a cat	bridge above it		
jumping	coldness	your mind	
from your hands	a shadow	stands	
	across its back	like a newborn	wolves walk
four soft pats		calf	the edges
on the sand	bears drop		of this heat
	salmon	the stabbing shock	
a constant	run from a	of perspective	the perfect circles
motion	different	is wildfire	of igloos melt
	darkness	through	
		the savannah	somewhere
			worms turn to eat
			their tails

The tips of your fingers

A slackening rain offers its small rhythm
to the rooftop, a soft shudder runs
through the house. On the radio,
Roethke is reading
of a woman he knew.
You are wearing
one of my shirts.

Now, I know it's no more
possible to own a moment
than a person, but sometimes
we can settle into one,
like a tide returning from the shore,
a soft relaxing back into the sea.

Wind slides the unlatched door
open, mist from the rain
catches the ends of your hair.
On the tips of your fingers,
my body seems achingly beautiful.

Today, we could begin to grow
back every limb we have lost.

The Drought

Your parents have come
and we have taken them to see
the botanical gardens.

Dried out from lack of rain,
only the succulents are thriving.

I point out the dragonflies
which I haven't seen for months
of city living, and spend too long
looking for frogs in the drying marsh.

On our way out, what look like waxwings
are swooping the little creek
that flows under the walking bridge.
Over our heads are the hungry waxwings,
swooping, and the insects we can't see.

Overhead are the waxwings,
hungry, and the swooping insects
and the questions we can't see.

The waxwings
the insects
and our questions
over our heads

swooping, hungry, we can't see.

Starstuff
[for three simultaneous voices]

It's hard for me to see a more profound cosmic connection than the astonishing findings of modern nuclear astrophysics: Except for hydrogen, all the atoms that make each of us—the iron in our blood, the calcium in our bones, the carbon in our brains—were manufactured in red giant stars thousands of light-years away in space and billions of years ago in time. We are, as I like to say, starstuff.
        Carl Sagan, *The Demon-Haunted World*

I.

these fractured scatterings
of stars shine like
seeds to a sparrow

if we could trust hunger
to be a true gateway
to desire
we could reap what we
could never sow

I.

these fractured collections
of atoms our bodies
meet like raindrops
colliding in air

if we could trust the simple
stars to collide we could
live inside this doubled
body

I.

if only we could stand back
we could see
the pattern
but we cannot stand back

if we could trust
in the pattern
we could learn to dance
this foolish tango
but we cannot
trust in the pattern

II.

her body is space
stationed in air
i swear
the mole
on her left breast
is a star
a galaxy
it was there that worlds
evolved
life
where life evolved
all thought
of God
of prayer
of obeisance

II.

my body is space
where there are no
planets to see

i am
that-without-orbit
foolish-man-kind
-ly-staring-at-stars

i am
that-which-nature-hates

i revolve
every gold star
i have licked
onto her body
in my mind
there are only
explorations

II.

planetary bodies
hide near those stars
shy prayers licked
tightly on their lips
just as the pollen
lurks around
her body
swirls
balletic orbits
in her lungs
there are only
exhalations

III.

she is a shining star
-tle
of gasp
our gods worship
every island
touch has placed
on her
    skin
holds their attention
they sleep with only
one eye shut

III.

and the gases twirled
into all life
our gods worship
this mapped dance
their footsteps glow
on the sky's
        black
                floor

III.

i pray
to whatever gods
our gods worship
do not take her
where the stars wink their
one eye shut

IV.

her voice on the phone
is meteor shower sizzle
through space
the husky perseids of my
desire
burn themselves
out in my throat

her voice on the phone
is

IV.

her voice her voice
her voice her voice
her voice her voice
her voice her voice
her voice her voice
her voice her voice
her voice her voice
her voice her voice
her voice her voice
her voice her voice
her voice her voice
her voice her voice
her voice her voice
her voice her voice

IV.

the black of the sky
is the   only
that makes us
notice the stars
shining brilliance
and the birds stay quiet
watching lost nests
appear through upper
branches
her voice on the phone
is lost to my voice

33

recitation
(4kl)

her breasts are like
green leaves   in spring

no   surely
i can do better than that

her legs are   like
the first sound of geese returning

from their wintered exile
no

her eyes are   like
humming

birds
hovering the lily

her breasts   her legs   her eyes
what thief would tell such extravagant lies

near her
i am the sabbath

the day god rested
and saw that it was good

our own concoction of red wine

sleeping, a door opens
and you want it you want it all in your
arms around the slender young waist of the
world in your arms like air screaming in your
silence of so many many songs in your
arms around the sugary flight of the bees
buzzing in your arms
around her.

Rembrandt: the artist as old man in love

I.
This unmarred canvas, my
wife, moves through the wind
like candlelight, all flicker and flutter.
I'm amazed she touches the earth
when she walks—I secretly
believe her footprints
are clever forgeries.

She saved me from my
lonely walk. I had been stumbling
for years, one more missed step
and I would have shattered into a thousand
worming pieces. She resurrected me.
My knees have grown supple
from my dreaming of her.

II.
A friend has told me of his travels
through Africa and India, has tried to convince me
to go. I have no need. Hendrickje
moves like an antelope,
a charging panther.
What I know of the circle of life
I've learned from the circle
of her hips, the dark continents
of her thighs. She is my well-spring
and I have lapped long, resting
in her shade. The shifting of her weight
is my tribal ritual, the source
of all my myths. Her legs are teeming

as the Ganges, her spine
is the mapless desert, tiny dune cresting
into dune.
        Together, we are the hunter
and the hunted. I have clawed her neck
on the grass plains of Africa,
she has opened my throat in India's
green jungles. We are each other's meat.
The gentle scent of her
through an open window hungers me.

III.
I have painted kisses on her
least parts, sculpted her inch by inch
with my lips. My body, wrinkled and soft,
takes on a firm outline in her hands.

She is all I know of dance, she is
my leap of grace. The smallest
movements of her hands
make the sparrows seem awkward.

a wet red rōz

ō mĭ luvs lĭk a wet red rōz
thats noolē drenchd ēch moon
ō mĭ luvs iz lĭk thuh furtil rān
that drips a darck maroon

az ritch art thow mĭ blēding lass
sō ful uv luv mĭ
nd yoo wil blēd thair stil mĭ dēr
til awl yr sēs run drĭ

til yr ōvarēs run drĭ mĭ dēr
nd yr egs r troolē dun
ō ĭ wil luv thē stil mĭ dēr
wen thuh rivr uv lĭf cant run

nd blēd thē wel mĭ ōnlē luv
nd blēd thē wel awĭl
nd wē wil cum agān mĭ luv
aftr thuh fludding uv yr nĭl

a neurosurgery course for non-neurosurgeons

I.
What colour were my hands
when they held your breasts,
so breathfull?

II.
Before you left, I told you
this world isn't perfect.

You said, *What bothers me is that*
it doesn't even try anymore—hell,
it stopped bathing centuries ago.

III.
The sunset plays its orange game of dice,
Venus keeps telling her off-colour jokes.
The dippers, the night's country & western records,
keep spinning like drunks around an old song.
Chaos theory is a nice fact tonight,
but where's the fluttering Japanese butterfly
to explain you?

IV.
You left with only a note on the fridge
saying *You're an asshole, a lousy lover,*
and a poetaster.

IVa. (The Poetaster's Haiku)
The words dropped from your
mouth like a wounded turkey.
Leave!Leave!Leave!Leave!Leave!

V.
All in all, she
was the dying wish
of a much kinder god.

Three Ghazals to the constellation Corvus (The Crow)

I

The woman was my gateway drug to bad poetry,
she sits in these words like a wound.

Snow peals back from the rocks,
a thousand dead nests on the ground.

Ravens sing their Spring love song,
crack the notes open to hear them bleed.

She is gone and I am healing:
always healing, never healed.

O Crow, life ain't about winning,
just losing as slowly as you can.

II

Birdshit hits rock, throws
open its loving arms.

Asshole, she called me, in her Stetson hat. Cowgirl,
I loved you and the horse you rode in on.

History is a predator,
the past is its prey.

41

Bird-thought, the stutter-step
into flying illumination.

O Crow, these women sit sober in the bar
and refuse to find me charming.

III

And what the hell is this,
fict or faction?

Her touch on my chest, simplicity—
the bend in the Raven's wing in flight.

Old scars bloom on my tongue.
I will not whisper her name.

Down the darkened alley, the streetlight
burns out as I walk by.

O Crow, up there silent in the sky, why
are you smiling?

I have learned few things

The man bends over to pick up the eel.
Before it is in the barrel, it is out of his hands
and back on the sidewalk.

The day is hot and humid in a city
I don't know well. The man in a white shirt
bends at the waist to pick up the coal black
line that won't stay straight or curved.
The eel is its own path
to nowhere. The barrel sits on the concrete
sidewalk, surrounded by the wet lashes
of a body drowning in air.

It is so hot and humid it is like swimming
I say. We walk through the Chinatown
of Toronto, a city I barely know. There is
an Asian merchant outside his shop
staring at an eel that won't go
into the bright yellow barrel filled with water.
The air is neither thick nor moist enough
for the eel to breathe but it refuses the man's hands
again and again. There is laughter. We turn the corner.

It is years later. No month has gone by without
the eel thrashing on the concrete sidewalk or the man
bending over, laughing, to pick it up again and again.

I turned the corner. The barrel filled with water
remains empty.

Seven Variations on the old Philosopher

1.
What is that silence?
Did i just not hear
a tree falling in the forest?

2.
There is you. Here is I.
A forest in between.
So many trees fall!

3.
The owl in flight.
The silent heart of the mouse.
Do the trees hear?

4.
Does a bear
shit in the woods?
Is that why the trees fall?

5.
The fallen tree.
The robins' bright
blue eggs . . .

6.
The trees all throw
their leaves in a pile.
Such a silly gamble.

7.
Hold my hand under this tree.
There is a silence
we must not miss.

for j. charles leblanc, 1919-2002

his breath.
a language ●
his lungs ●
can/no
longer read

cells outgrowing their walls.
2/3 water.
duST.
Dust.
dUst.

Earth receive rest.

Gone, that gentle night.

The unleaved goldengrove.

We are left to console the sides of wet stones.

it was a hot day the windows closed and blinds drawn to keep the sun
out put my head on kelly's chest strongly heard the strong muscle
beating blood to her arms that held me / goodbye.

Ten
(for rob mclennan)

ten the spots places or the held longer best card

tenacious memory quality surgical etc. a ditch tenant the estate

tenant farmer a state coastal teleostean flesh take stand with

tend to think fast result quality something as vessel larger

tender one's obligation a formal work services tender chewed pain

tenderfoot scout easily past or undercut device fruit consisting muscle

tendril coil to the candles exposure light a civilization preceding

tenement rents in divided section miles highest market and principle

tennessee usa between valley dairy phosphates and ceded chief knoxville

tennis oath separate king assembled inflammation
                                        use hand chiefly published

My ignorance of Mina Loy

The immaculate
conception
of the inaudible bird
occurs
in gorgeous reticence . . .
                    —Mina Loy

1.

the declivity of the mind
into ambiente putrefaction

is this a baedeker
or just parturition

2.

amative coquette kohls her eyes
the aniline in the air enervates our breviaries

in the vestry, sarsenet mitre is postulated
with avidity, infructuous agamogenesis
almost carnose in the cyclamen

the antipodean question silences the loquent

3.

Quadrille disorbs the haulms,
cymophanous petals etiolated
by the footle and flummery

caryatid supports the entablature
with all her legerdemain

the sacerdotal eremite's eclosion
is ended for the night

4.

Scissioned by the horologe
a baldachined parvenu,
innubile, gravid with fondant
obtunds the intestate day's sere solfeggio

For the inamoratos
there is only effulgent suttee.

Stellar Cartography

I thought about stars and clichés—shimmering, cold, perfect dead images.

I thought about a planet too far from the sun to hold life, and the small, dark mole on her hand.

I thought about Polaris, the creatrix, how it will spin out of the centre long after we die.

I thought about history and time, about the dulled knife we use to cut through them.

I thought about the night sky as the breast of a mother crow warming her nest, her feathers shimmering in a sheen of light rain.

I thought about a bird in flight, flickering between light and shadow, about dust creeping into a timepiece and slowly slowing the second hand.

I thought about the sun burning itself out.

I thought about galaxies forming from dust, long spiral arms whirling in a mad dance.

I thought about the backs of her knees, how the wind swirled in those two shallow cups like twin galaxies of desire.

I thought about long nights of regret stretching behind me, and I thought about milk and honey, bread falling from the sky.

I thought about the sun, the moon, their constant spin towards eclipse.

I thought about animals fooled into night-thoughts and then a dazzling, mid-sky sunrise.

I thought about her hair, how it burst from her head like a blinding solar collision.

I thought about the time she fell asleep with stickers of stars stuck to her cheeks.

I thought about the faint grey of the least visible stars, about the other stars we can't see at all.

I thought about those who first mapped the moon, how they looked away from the earth and found the Bay of Rainbows, the Sea of Tranquillity, looked to the stars and saw stories.

I thought about the staccato of stars as a hard, brail language of grief, and I thought about the staccato of stars as the refined liquefaction of joy, cresting slowly over us all.

I thought about offering six lines of wonder:

one: the stars hanging over us like petals, like beads of a lover's sweat, like notes in our marvellous, personal operas.

two: the stars as tiny nightlights God has reached back into our room to turn on to keep the bad dreams away.

three: a crescent moon, the perfect simplicity of its shape, like the precise curve of her fingernails after she bathed in the morning.

four: the stars as every baseball Hank Aaron hit out of the park.

five: the stars as a series of angels' bare asses, pressed against heaven's car window, the moon as God's naked reminder not to take it all too seriously.

six: the stars as a field of wet wheat, rustled by a summer prairie wind, bobbing their heads and shushing each other, spellbound by it all, by everything, the pulsing beauty of life.

I thought about the seventh line, always waiting.

I thought about space travel and Hawking's wheelchair, and a squirrel I once saw, leaping.

I thought about men trapped in metal, miles above the earth.

50

I thought about how, to them, the earth itself must be like a dream forgotten at the moment of waking.

I thought about the way her hips wiggled, so unlike anything I can see in the sky.

I thought about constellations, and satellites streaming through them with no one to chart the new, fleeting patterns they make.

I thought about the thin blue veins in the back of my hands, the network of blood we can only imagine.

I thought about the dragonfly's thin, delicate wings, how we can never quite see them in flight.

I thought about the Pleiades, shimmering, about rain hitting flowering peonies like perfect seeds of diamonds, and I thought about that look in her eyes.

I thought about Venus, low in the evening sky.

I thought about seeing a bird standing on the rivershore, about walking closer and startling it into flight so I could name it—Heron.

I thought about why an unknown bird standing on the rivershore under a star-filled sky wasn't enough.

I thought about fireflies, their whirling, unmappable constellations, and I thought about her, about my fingers when they circled the small of her back.

And I thought about stars.

Two

were the *bees*

were the bees
(A Dance with Duncan)

> The dancer comes into the dance when he loses his consciousness
> of his own initiative, what he is doing, feeling or thinking, and enters the
> consciousness of the dance's initiative, taking feeling and thought there. The
> self-consciousness is not lost in a void but in the transcendent consciousness
> of the dance. . . . As consciousness is intensified, all the existing weave of
> sensory impression, the illustration of time and space, are "lost" as the
> personality is "lost"; in focus we see only the dancer. We are aware only
> in the split-second in which the dance is present. This presentation, our
> immediate consciousness, the threshold that is called here-and-now and
> eternity, is an exposure in which, perilously, identity is shared in resonance
> between the person and the cosmos.
>   —Robert Duncan, "Towards an Open Universe"

> The hive of human being: it is this in part we work in composing. Poets, we
> hear languages like the murmuring of bees. Swarm in the head. Where the
> honey is stored. An instinct for words where, like bees dancing, in language
> there is a communication below the threshold of language.
>
> There is a natural mystery in poetry. We do not understand all that we
> render up to understanding.
>   —Robert Duncan, "Pages from a notebook"

1.

Last night during your reading
of characteristic later odes,
my idea was of resonances between phrases:
a city cannot return anything; and *in America of course
you don't need a word like eternity*.

science is always advancing new pictures of what the universe is;
for me (although I read it along oppositions that were felt)
Marx reduces things to economies—and Freud reduces
letters in which she says *you know*,
as I came back from Mallorca and

something; they were filled with domestic scenes,
Williams's letters. Pound said, "Oh, he comes in just mad after all
hive." So the bee dance still draws me. But then we're never drawn;
each man is a law unto himself and
has to be the proposition he is.

When you're not engaged with the field,
the walking,
boy, you get screwed in the trap because
every being (and we're back to law) has its own law. if
you do not have the occurrence happening
deep, the *fact* that
you feel preside over
feeling,
of course you won't believe that
we have magic obscurities in
the expression
not "lost" but seeking other levels of engagement.

2.

The Pisan Cantos and the first books of *Paterson*
I suppose we gave
to read aloud.   And then from that breakthrough
vast needs were made,
and a hatred of the word eternity. You
planned a little book called *In Homage to Coleridge*,
with the paraphernalia of contemporary
doctoring he hated.
ideas in books; these were not bees and
beehives—the atrocity that people do in the beehive!
His dogma was
the line is moving,
every level philosophically appearing, because
often you miss its message, it was the other one; but then
any law, every
happening in letters
always brings you right to that level, because
to form
myself there's a question
I wouldn't think to ask. this is the task. We must remember
Hart Crane; come close
talking about direct
ideas of a rhapsodic poem or elegy.

3.

And so going toward a dramatic center,
he's got to have his, he's got to
feel the time. Yet I'm immensely conservative of
you, a classical example.
We got outside of our own
interchanges of language.
in straight voice, what good is
the contemporary world? I sent them off to blast
it at somebody. Of course this is in St. Elizabeth's,
in a child, in gardens where
beehives similar to the cream of the
Heraclitian God read
my early rhetoric that I was ashamed of. I came
diagraming the Now. beyond the diagram,
you ain't got no metaphysic, and
I'm convinced it ain't just one or another, there is one
tune that poets of every level conceive.
They're very awkward,
so strict about keeping to the business of the poem.
God makes all things simultaneously
obscure to *him*, only if the word blocks his knowing.
Open the way to a new kind of
form. So my breakthrough came

4.

The key, the shifting, is
everything, the whole thing going,
a massive conversion to understand the earth
in our own translations.
I knew well that so beautiful
language where angry
beehives watched the process.
But neither Russia nor
Heraclitus had it all
near to reciting.
The diagram, the space for
writing the great reaction was
you, and this is our beehive,
this struggling to know
the sub-dictionary meaning,
the simultaneity, the reason that there is
all this countryside

5.

Now that's the kind of thing
I'm not going to take. I'm not going
around the sun instead of the sun going around the earth.
We were mistrusted, we were put down.
A poet frequently will write the high
beautiful thing, about that I was not wrong at all.
I have never written, nor did I ever
talk about
collecting honey,
for
we share in the world.

                                              i mean,
all the women in purple
would say he isn't truly spatial. But, conceptually, he is spatial.
His books get rid of learning and yet are
endlessly creative of message. This seems to me the essential
tune of law. He may be
the syllable, the powerhouse.
who really wants to be the voice of the unconscious?
I talk about myself, about a sense that
meaning *is* because we are sitting
and the word is the place where I think it. In
times obscure,
what was your reaction to time?
What was really going on was
the poem, itself its content of ideas, embodied
co-existence of all things in it.

6.

take the closed, the open, because I want
that conversion, you, a conversion of form,
co-existence of such
manner.
His property would be
my whole life; that was an inspiration,
the kind of hostility you find in autobiography.
Apprehensive because you might be stung,
I gasp with horror as we turn
like mermaids,
truly engaged in space, always
within a period of turning. Suddenly
language becomes so excited that
every thing is flowing back to that syllable.

Frequently this is part of the picture,
a reminder that
now is simultaneous in each of our centers.
Believe the word, present it
to me.

Reason would pose there are two kinds of
form, I
said. Charles threw himself down on the lawn,
poet belonging to the lore of poetry.

entirely a conversion of what man is, of what earth is,
very strong against the very good reason
between two areas. Freud brought us to look at
the things my mind engaged,
the kind of cat I am. His property would be
vengeance; I wrote
shots of it. it was unfair to
you, the
bee at the center.

Sirens call like the sea
to be engaged in an art of space,
suddenly getting to cold hell, which opened up
endlessly creative of message.
You tried to make the
going yours, not mine, you
refer to the superiority
of this big unconscious Id. out of the
thing alive—
everything we could be. Only in the
yielding, a meaning,
rather than the meaning of
closed and open certainty.
Experience is startling
questions. One of the decisive things

8.

not rhetorical but rhetoric itself, the equivalent
language of the insane and the language
that he dedicates.
It was quite clear to me how
to write: no. American. language. I wrote
the autobiography of ill and the autobiography
honey draws from the hive. tag along, see
the social termite colony with its vast queen who
proves a Siren. I look like a
painting, you'll find; I mean you will find
an important aspect
begins to be limited in message, and finally people
have their own contents.
If you take the whole intoxicating spell
of artists, my count of them is
water,
because I also mean. In some part of my own
simultaneous creative existence we have
vast poetics.
They themselves
brought
startling sight of this *thing* advancing,.
of what sun is, and this is enough

9.

area dismissed as non-sense,
a part of the dedication,
biography belonging to illness. His was a character
smoked out, or a picnic when somebody hits a hive
and all the working termites
are hideous, though with sweet voices
engaged in space.
force of the process as a process of transforming
the message.

That may be *au natural.*
Maybe I'll get back to the fine distinctions misleading
us and recover, dis-cover actual being,
introduce the meaning that
presents such obscurities. He feels
projective to me,
a fundamental difference in structure. So it was
we were already
level, lying flat on the ground—we talked
enough to convert any art form. it's simply a feeling of
blasphemy (other dirty words could be used)

when I came,
I was miscellany
throughout. you find this increasing
part of the beeworld:
psychic extensions have their being in her.
He concentrates on dogma; he concentrates
psychology into something that is energy.
Endlessly creative of message, that one sense
giving birth to
our studies of language.

It isn't entirely the art of
negative capability swimming ashore.

I have the thing that moves the unknown
person to person.
Believe there are only two.
people
are rhetorical
non-sense? There was no non-sense in Freud.

tradition is clear enough, especially when you
print at my expense. in
increasing part, the autobiography composes
me. summers when I was perhaps.
The idea of individuality
concentrates much on the ritual, the dance. I had
the field, I
measured space all the time.
Great messages
always get sent by
content.
Study language or general principles,
I must be viewed as
the concert's apprehension of
sleep not discovered. Being a poem, I
asked him to explain a poem. What
alternates between things that are not enigmatic.
I don't think a third alternative
was observed as late as our time—the sun goes
in arms along with sky.

12.

We are not interested in the justice of a poet,
in the hills in Santa Barbara, in this beautiful
individuality that has law to itself.
A round dance puts into means
a spatial consideration,
sonnets at the very beginning of sonnets.
Instance observably does not come from
the structure of ideas; the thing broke through
and I'm strongly, strongly persuaded
when you are thinking of the entire
actuality of form, it is
meaning, we find, that explication dodges.
Enigmatic at this level, the things in him
are catching
little phrases with commas.

If there is a field
around the earth, we will figure as matter,
a connection in regard to
clear thinking.
The two of these
have many little keys.

or the ratio to other
garden of my mother, where there was sage along the
larger course, for me. That's the
terms of tradition of place.
From what you have said, what I know of
defining space. On the stage it
had energy and resource for construction and concept.
The fact in such states of excitement.
Jackasses want to stuff things into things as if that were the event,
studies in linguistics, which I
became converted to. I'm not certain reading
poetry is consciousness, but
you are holding it extremely crude.
The indwelling and discovering
give the explication: you account for your words,
walls will present themselves.
He used this term with its double
citizenship
of all in one. I saw that I serve within
fact; so much does the sun rise and sink in my
walls, in
Eros and Thanatos.
Were all writing in quatrain forms,
there were other things. There is another
writing—and wrote at great length

slope of the hill towards the harbour, thick with bees,
the cosmos, finally. There I would be
years, or something like that; express it
in terms of time.
When I was concerned with certain
relations of things, my impressions would be
that language is incapable of
tuning out the event.
And then we ransacked the same linguists—oh,
now I have the feeling of superiority, but
everything manifests the minute's sounded
spell,
the form that's there. We sometimes
account for all our acts. Life
presents absolute walls of this kind; I'm
becoming interested in the
play of voice when you read
this business of eternity, in
the few places\where Galileo has entered
what the words mean. How can you hope to know
the two great, creative forces in the universe, Eros
and derivative thought?
The door was part of the dedication.
He did not go wild about
reality

my cosmos is clearly
a kind of emblem of the entire
sense in which time is your basic concept
of space.
Much reaction goes toward creating energy and
producing message. In those two things, wonder,
which is the real thing, is a great misunderstanding.
I read, after the fact, of
decisions I recognize
belong to consciousness, and here the words'
fineness of distinction leaves them floundering.
We are very
hung up on accounting for,
and won't go further in the account
of origin. Guess was the issue,
loud and deep in the idea of the imagination.
Whatever I made of composition,
I have come deeply immersed in its various
feeling of form; striking me,
the words conceal
Thanatos. Later readings would be sexual readings.
Read them. I derive all my forms from adoration.

In Mallorca, Creeley was fascinated
and I think the last real correspondence came then,
the autobiography. He saw the creative complex that
courses, could see there were different kinds of bees: bumblebees

16.

concentrate on what it means,
that box and so forth; my sense of space
feels always a lack, unsatisfied in the
either/or I'm in. There are times when we find
initiation of the thing, and
recognize, but can't do.
My fingertips are my consciousness. It
becomes very important to bring oneself to order, because you
could never come to the place where
writing
is a projection in relation to the world.
I was working on the
field instance, as far as I can read and figure
ratifications, and many different
feelings of that whole event
would be structures of
adoration and falling in love with my mind,
fascinated by White Goddess ideas. They
couldn't tell male from female.
These irritations are extremely petty
in the cosmos; and absolutely like language

17.

to be able to show
the level of time's terms in the
dimensions of creation and resource . . . It emerges that he is unsatisfied.
I had read Whorf, and often I
recognize what's happening, it
might or might not be in the mind. I talk about
misleading the audience; you are misleading yourself
as a matter of fact.
What does breakthrough remains symbolic;
something has moved off,
following the poetry. It was
easy to read in our rhetorical and elegiac
Medieval period,
seeing sun not rising or sinking, but earth turning.
Oh yes, the walls fall when
creative structures come close to poetry and
transform into part of the picture.
Male, female,
and personal reappear in that autobiography related to
bees, big wooly ones, little busy ones, and so
cosmos; and certainly in that I'm interested

18.

I don't write the poem; I'm not dealing with the
satisfied creation of
the Human Universe.
The one we're tuned in on
was sophisticated at the linguistic
prohibition, a closed-off
fineness of distinction and discretion; talk
a counterpost to *that*.
Sometimes the poet writes sense,
so hung up on making a bridge that he can't
gear his immediate presence.
The one that was impossible to read
made some reference to
the power.
Eternity is the field, that point of
the earth turning
out life and letters.
Sex was creative, it was not merely
mastery of the form. I could
woman the structure of poetry.
Bees must
divine
and draw it in space. So I don't think

19.

That means from society,
city and ideas of polis; all those were
important when composing.
linguistic level could be very perverse, could beat me
towards using words that way—yet intellectually it
is about control. Drive the car, conscious,
because they have conscious engagement in themselves.
What does it mean that I'm making a bridge?
Shifting gear toward a new form was the first
ecology.
Certain principles are suggestive and cannot be exhausted;
eternity interferes because that isn't what it means. So there is
the level of what we were taught,
and also the time (in the late 3os) when I got
sexual. You could take—some Freudians did—the genital organs.
It must have come from immersing himself in
the muselike goddess.
Making that woman,
we have the slightest disagreement, men have;
it almost turns you negative-positive.
Space and time are far apart, but
co-existence and simultaneity of parts appear to be chronological

20.

supercharged with creative meaning,
directing the syllable,
that tic tac toe
comes as this terrific charge,
the time of delight
bridging two unbridgeable things,
heart to the beat, and breath to the syllable.
Reading as a savage
interest.
We wrote
eternity as time's
language rising and sinking. Language
most of the people
and you find the universe is
other people.

It is constant in my mind that there are bees
burned happily. The lamp extinguished because
you find its antithesis
is unsatisfied with energy

the immediate sub-dictionary event
was obsessed, was incapable of moving
visual work in its potencies. I don't feel
the best dimension is the same
Heavenly City.
accounting for
the physiological thing is a
savage form of terminal.
Exploit the countryside
called composition. I took much
to be other than it is, but a field of time reveals the pathway.
Language is conservative of its
co-ordination; the cosmos proves to be
decisions of the terminal: the decision between
the drones and the queen, the feeding
of the heresy. involved disagreement
had been presumed before we met.
My prejudice would have me as a
resource of the cosmos. That can be profoundly disturbing.

22.

simply dissolve into time;
the "can't" is like a prohibition
over your shoulder while you read.

was botched, was refusing to face
why the poem is his major potency. But a potency
accounting for what they are,
not reflecting how much would change.
terminal junctures should have been a hint—
systems grow political and cultural coercion.
returned again and again, today
as a path in now.
co-existing forms thank God; this is how
ideas mean—a
terminus and beginning of another so similar.
there was an offensive difference and distance between
the love lives of
queens. At early age they
lay down dogma. read it without knowing
your question. certainly the
problem has to do with
Space versus Time,
the real poetics, and this is very much
hung up on the thing you were saying before

23.

I take as much as I can, I tune up
the exquisite pleasure in little. it's
important because my concept
has not arrived at this being, I
operate by the fact that it obscures itself.
Meaning has forced me back.
the farmer has a corps of
projective interpretations,
a different physics.
We try to capture
something else in the period
of graves.
What made possible
the various,
the special food, the beefood?
At every turn your favorite adversary or heretical little
breakthrough into writing the definite
structure of occurrences; the major problems are
the physical level. And of course, observably,
let's say we have
lost a lot of ground—well, what do we do,
my obsession?

24.

After all, you are taking pleasure in these decisions.
Form is the co-inherence of all parts and all other parts,
but, when I go back, language always is a
present to us. And when you find
a very strong force,
have in mind the kind of rhetoric which
is already articulating small phrases.
Who convinces
change, its powerful suggestion? Its principles
are formed beyond the field. I was picturing
those cave walls as we imagine
Marxism, which is exactly the same in this regard
—I would when presented
with the thing
decide to leave this out of the transcript.
Put in that the bee develops as a bee developing
the course of drama.
If you look at just the
ecology of time you
have physical difficulties.
Particles in their possibilities,
so potent when you go to the sub-dictionary event that is
a fuse going toward fate;
it is correction

25.

poem, I've got to increase my memory and recognition of
event; language is taking advantage. You see you have to see
or else you're asked the question about
San Francisco. That rhetoric was out of line,
was based on jazz and I
need a fur coat with the food.
Principles go much further
picturing
their terms are their own universe.
look at what's happening in history,
the alternatives of the closed and open
event,
stumbling after the muse,
developing as a worker or a drone. The sexual composition of
dogma—
I was 18,
exempted from the draft because of "night sweats." I mean, really.
Immensely productive of self, whole poetries
bewildered, and she does not believe that
correction, that
his howl is silent

when things are immensely
you, suddenly you're giving an account of it, that's
academic. To be upon the page and
not a listener of jazz; the syncopations came from
my prototype of the Russian Revolution.
Going to Maximus has by no means exhausted the actual
pathways of events.
we rightly read in terms that have layers.
You ask what does it *mean*, what does it *mean* that
one side is presented intellectually,
moving away from form to time—the subtle
fool stumbling after the White Goddess is
himself quite hot about the
hive; your polis and civitas
are Roman Catholic. As for
expectancy, it's hard to recapture now, to
engage in a spatial construct—they are probably flat.
Time enters
abnormal conditions into a normal nervous system.

flowed out of this, we were writing away; most
sense lies in the sub-dictionary-level
distinctions, and I find a reprimand in that
howl. He is a Ginsberg in a way, but of course his
every single particle is different from the same

last night, an account of
reflective in language,
different area of music. The tone of
revolution, the first sign of the fact that the
force of his seeing can see a form as a field of things.
Some got physics,
layers of a picture of a world. A field isn't
proletariat, and what does a depression *mean*?
My Heraclitian feeling is kept alive,
ardently wanting to appreciate the opposite
of talk. What is a citizen?
Us romanticists, our whole tradition was to
think and follow a melodic line,
not some
example where you go back and back and
carry "meaning"; you will find the responses
constantly, because this is not an anti-type but something
silent. The delicacies of decisions must be
the most crude level of what
charged the poem itself.

28.

I was not quick to pick up on
the new Regime, as much a police state as
the development of a path
—convinced that particles are individuals
you progress from right ideas to wrong ideas,
and then an entirely different
structure of you takes me.
The form I expected
undoes you, leaves you stumbling and crippled.
In your
complexion the bee-hive is the prototype,
nothing, nothing, nothing; nothing
engaging in a spatial construct.
I did not know before; it was not until
symptoms, body symptoms. I don't think you can
refresh your mind with the resources of science,
it may only come from
the vast sentiment
that is needed at the crucial point of the
admired. The refinement, the microscopic decision.
melody.
I find myself incapable of
not trying to get that person close

be an example of rhetoric
read aloud in
the Tzarist Regime, Trotsky requisitioning food from
immense change in form. I was talking last night
from wrong ideas to right ideas,
dynamics of history moving;
time to bring back my
subdued castration.
the bee dance suggests something
of the matriarchal state in the human mind.
my parents believed
in America, a
kind of confidence highly disturbed by
1956 San Francisco. he had,
without realizing, almost a proto-Reichian body,
an inkling of
the potency in the atomic explosion
of ought and ought not to do.
where you make fine
superiority an art, the vastness of power does not see
form in the co-inherence of all parts;
their sensibility has poetic "effect,"
but you're actually trying to escape yourself

3o.

a point of poetic:
Ukraine didn't get a damn thing from Moscow.
Trying to picture time
blasts open the
progress from right ideas to wrong ideas.
To find a dialectic, he has to
shame the old rhetoric of earlier forms. My
movement was
injured, a stumbler, and practiced stumbling
with admiral
quality of language.

They were identical,
dominated by vast and inert mediocrities, appalling
advances into
Reality.
Disorder
emerged at the level
of particles.

I find my decisions very crude.

I more and more question
our developed awareness
in the expanded poetic

Three

Small Moons: Ghazals

its autumn   and leaves are turning
our footprints   into sound

no one moves   freely now
every step   is charted   on its axis   deliberate   cold

the botanist sees   the organic whole
the hunter watches   for the rustle   in the bushes

robins   flitter in   the oaks
a fire that doesnt   consume   itself

the trees   outside your   window
claimed   your lungs   in the name of   lilac

relax   little mind   there are no   great epiphanies here
only   a few leaves   still clinging   to the trees

bunkered deep   inside me in   the old lizard
brain   i suppose youre   still there

on the radio   another codependant lovesong   dances
you   across my animal   mind   in duple time

foxthought your way   back to me
my dark   plathy   darling

a frightened cub sees   the world outside   its den
as one giant   orchestration   against its mothers return

the music spikes   as the cat   jumps   out from the dark   and you relax
into the knife

i poke at you   like a scab on my knee or   to be honest
can i be honest   with you   yet   like a scar on my old lizard

i stand   watching the women dance   like a man developing
strangers photographs

whats inside me   a poor poet would say in the heart in the blood but i a poor
drunkard think it hides in my liver   could be a whirling dervish.

even my cat   is more drinking   partner than pet
she mewls   for aspirin in the morning

in the bar again   and im not looking for a woman
to keep up with me   just one   wholl put up with me

the old jokers   never go out of style   henny youngman
take my life   please

damn you john thompson
damn you   and your itchy   trigger finger

she walked by a bush and it   burst
into flame   sparrows wings

a bullet can   pass   through only
so many   bodies   before it stops

my mind craves her   like narrative
her lack   is the start   of my stories

noah called the animals   two by two
the dove   was a fool   to return

life   keeps dropping the soap
i   keep bending over to pick it up

it is a january night   even the smallest
birds   have left   my feeder

a bible   bound   in human skin
her body holds   all my commandments

she is here but   impossible to   believe in
like a dolphin   dead by drowning

we topped the hill   and the moose shuffled off the road
ran beside the car   like . . . no.   like . . . no.   like . . . and then gone

my hands fall   open
like a book   of mourning

hank williams   no show jones   sit down and have a beer
before you play your   final set

a black   cat   crossing everyones path
my body has   no fixed address

(4kl)

i mouth   something   into your belly
more than words   pool in your navel

now   just where the hell did you come from
dear god   your buildings named shangri *la*

de da   my friends say   but sometimes
life is   even wankier than poetry

moonshine   and these milkwrapped   dunes
your naked back   in the bed beside me

whodve thought id   find some sexualspiritualthang
baby   if the korans a rockin . . .

so here i am   the dyslexic blues   singer finally
unemployed   by all this   happi fuckingness

(4kl)

paul says   for a poet   falling in love
is an occupation   al hazard

the trainwreck   unexpected
ly rerailed   rescue crews stand   scratching their heads

i have lived   in three   time zones   sir
sanford fleming   brought me   to you

like the water   droplet   ive been held
together   by only my   tension

riding through   the desert
lawrence dreams   his arabia

the cat sleeps   on your chest
with one eye   opened

the order breaks   down now
this folk tale   always ends   in tears

septembers   a month of   science
not laughter

we each have our questions   for god
we all   get the same response   in the end

a lump   her breast
what soliloquies   would hamlet have for this

we each have   the same response   god
for   in the end   all   we   get our questions

a month of   septembers
not   science   laughter

down breaks   the tale   now this order
    ends folk   in tears   always

onsleeps   cattheeyeone with
   your   chest   opened

here we are   like a bridge   under   troubled wat/DONT SAY IT   christ
never a disgruntled postal employee   around   when you need one

me n j. b. gettin ready for the big   payback
we dont know karate   but we do know   karazy

the time sheet says six on   one off   but how
many days rest   did he need   my love   after creating you

shiva   does his dance   of destruction   blood
must have its course   and every god   his prey

o sure   i can turn   a phrase till its dizzy
but sometimes i forget   am i zager or evans

three months later   she calls me   handsome
learning to judge   this cover by its book

the deaf man knows   only one
use for his tongue

i should stop my   bitching   and get on with it
really   who cares   about tichbornes elegy

im no wink martindale   but this dating game   isnt so easy
even if im fain   in verse my love to show

ah for chrissake   if it aint unfixed
dont broke it   stupid

my lady   with the milk   cold legs enters the room
old man time gets all cock   eyed

your lover lies next to you   with a headache
youve forgotten   the words to the lords prayer

the clock is all sfumato   our conversations   like a scar
we cover   with makeup

an intellectual   youd stop writing   these ghazals if only
you could learn   how

what argument   pollock   can you offer
against the radial   balance   of her breasts

i reach after answers   as the candlelight   slips
down   the further   and harder it stretches

sure   bill   but can we know   the runner   from the run
the driver from the drive   maybe the writer from the right

and so you   think   its up to you   poetboy
with your experimental   sincerity   ?

a eulogy for me   ah christ
try a stiff   glass of drink

this old earthball   can spin   a wild ride my friends
watch the men   with   no questions

as a child   mother took
my hand   and held on

(2 for the greenboathouse)

a washroom and a   gift shop
where they drove in   the last spike

outside the city   the stars know you
as well as   heraclitus

the late   night collectcall
is the drunkards   sonnet sequence

what wooden   train tunnel
will save you   from this   avalanche

who looked at the stars
and felt   the need   for narrative

here i am too   drunk to see the forest
fire for all   the trees

o bacchus   youd think id notice   the embers
burning two holes   in the crotch   of my pants

the morning after   waking up in a little slice of bc paradise
jasons asleep   robs still drunk   mike searches the firepit for his glasses

the quail and the ducks make short work
of our leftovers   regrets and promises

a couple gaze   at the mountains   for a photo
touched   by the moments   aweinspiring   cliché

like i told rob   if you ever   see me jogging   start running yourself
theres something   really bad   behind me

driving through the mountains   the big horns   are only an   obstacle
proof   that even lovers   must have moments   of reason

no one knows   what   theyll be doing   in ten years but
the lucky ones   have a good idea   who

in the right light   even   broken
          glass caresses   the rainbow

your arm   on my bare   chest while   the stars
darkle   that is all   i know   of time

monks   mad   from sexless   years
the salmon   throw   themselves   at the bears

finally   can set down   pencil and eraser   ive stumbled
on a plan   proof enough   for this fool

your chest   rising and falling   in the bathwater
what olive branch   i will carry   from this   solid   ground

go ask   lucretia   how many men need   be struck
dumb   by the soup   steaming before them

the pianos already   know every song   that will be written
we stumble   through   the notes   one   by one

as clear   water can leave   no trace
your tongue   on the lobe of my ear

does this pen   of mine   have enough   shakespeare
to keep her   young   forever

so tell me   godiva how many men have been dumb
struck   by the sweat   streaming   in the small of your back

(in drumheller alberta)

a weekend   in drumheller   oh no
daddy   wont be taking   my   t bird away

fred   barney   this   is where   youve been hiding
dragging hairy   knuckles   to your pick ups   and taverns

so al   where do you get   that wife when   you cant
put even   your thumbs   in the earth

looking out   8o feet high   from the mouth   of the fibreglass
t rex   i can see my   error   most clearly

wise oedipus   riddle me this   if i didnt   want
to leave   would   all   the stoplights   still   burn red

we   look   at the stars   lost
but still   flickering   above us

what   prodigal   myths   must be   spoken   of earth
in the darker   parts   of space

here   we are   stuck   in the present   tense
a distance   between   us   more than   physical

how quickly we   set aside   our he man   fantasies
and start dreaming   of becoming post   master   of the universe

love you   and i   will soon be   riddles of the past   no   more
than painted hands   pressed together   on walls of rock

in the daylight   a half   moon shines   through
from another   sky neither   more   or less   darkened than ours

(st valentines day 2002 4kl)

o wise men   of science   can you not see   how the stars   shine now
on her   who is to me   the messiah

your appearance in my song   most   prodigal of lovers
caught   this petty solomon   sorely   off   his guard

for all to hear   i am   the man who wanders   proudly
by your side   whispering   shibboleth   shibboleth

a poor biblical scholar   i study you   my bounty
to seek wisdom   on the miracle   of the loaves and the fish

revisionists everywhere   alter the order   of creation   no god
they say   could wait   six days   with dreams of   you   in his head

i know little   of the things i know   but this i know   too well
a razorblade   is a poor   dance partner

the mapmakers   know fear
and love   as matters of geography

the empty chair   doesnt miss   the absent sitter
the empty   bed doesnt   miss the sleeper

what a poor   piece of furniture
this heart

ghalib   i can carry both   ends of this   conversation
for only   so long

sooner or   later death grasses   us away
the final mystery   always a green one

overhead   the waxwings   flit   from tree to tree
such tiny needles   stitch a forest   to the sky

the straw   berry rests   on my tongue
like the nipple of spring

the world staggers   to a strange   dance
step   my love   while bach   is in the air

midnight   her bare feet   silent on the floor
how can this   not be   a threat

the wind warps   to your will   my love   you are the first
bird   in a world   of archeopteryx

icarus   there is a reason we   werent   given wings   who
wouldnt fly   from this ball   of dirt

when the dove   came back   the water
was still deep   enough to   drown you

did bacon write   shakespeare   ah love
in a thousand years even   this kiss   will be a matter of doubt

o weaver   im beginning to think   that your trick
has   only one   pony

(an early birthday present)

the leaves   on the   ground tree
tongues still wet   from eating light

down past the navel   o   that deep
romantic   chasm

at the end   what   is left   the thievery
a lock   pick breaking into   song

distance her   goldened
ratio   with my mouth

above stars   speak their maudlin   desire
red shift   red shift   red shift

samuel   im in love   why   have you brought me
just another fucking   romantic sublime

so there i am   always the new   pool boy
but   never   in the right   film

grief   around her   a small moon
all i see   is the dark   side

all is perspective   perhaps   what we need
now   is barbaric   poetry

in the field   two paint   horses licking the back
of each   others   neck

o ghalib   in the end
the truth   is in   the putting

Notes

"My ignorance of Mina Loy" takes words found throughout Loy's poetry; the vast majority of these words were ones I was ignorant of and had to look up in the dictionary.

"Were the Bees" is a cut-up sequence based on George Bowering and Robert Hogg's 1969 interview of Robert Duncan (Beaver Kosmos, 1971). A base text was formed by taking the corresponding line from each page of the interview (for example, the base text for the first piece contained the first line from each page, the second base text contained all the second lines, etc.). I then removed words from the base text until the piece voiced its own concerns.

Acknowledgments

Portions of Duncan's interview reproduced with the permission of the Literary Estate of Robert Duncan, along with the permission of Robert Hogg and George Bowering.

Some of the poems in this book have appeared in the following journals:
The Fiddlehead
Grain
NewWest Review
Prairie Fire
Queen's Quarterly
Qwerty
Shampoo (US)
as well as in the chapbooks *other work for your hands* (above/ground press, 2004) and *not knowing spanish*(Greenboathouse, 2002) and the anthology *Evergreen: 6 new poets*, edited by rob mclennan (Black Moss, 2002).

"Ten" appeared in the above/ground press collection *Ten*, which commemorated the tenth anniversary of rob mclennan's loving domination of the Canadian small press scene.

"Three Ghazals to the constellation Corvus (The Crow)" appeared as a chapbook of the same name from above/ground press in 2001.

My thanks to the editors of all the above.

I would also like to thank the Alberta Foundation for the Arts for providing several writing grants that were instrumental in the completion of this collection.

Thank Yous

My sincerest thanks to Jan Zwicky, who has taught me more about writing poetry than anyone else.

My thanks to everyone who helped with the shaping of these poems. Steve McOrmond and Paul Dechene, in particular, both provided invaluable insight and editorial suggestions. rob mclennan has offered and continues to offer a tremendous amount of support. Doug Barbour's enthusiasm and friendship have been more important to me than he could possibly know. Adam Dickinson—walker, cartographer, man about town—has provided me with many hours of discussion on poetry that have been entertaining, challenging, frustrating, and always illuminating. Robert Bertholf, Robert Hogg, and George Bowering were extremely kind (and trusting) in granting me permission to use the Duncan interview as I have. Many thanks for friendship and encouragement to Bill Gaston, Eric Hill, Don McKay, Dave Seymour, Sue Sinclair, Murray Sutcliffe, and Matthew Tierney, all of whom offered support when the seeds of this collection were first planted.

Kelly Laycock has played both muse and first ear to most of the poems in this book; just as I would not be who I am without her, so this book would not possibly be what it is without her many efforts. All my love and deepest thanks.

ANDY WEAVER was born in Saint John, New Brunswick, and grew up there, Ottawa, Ontario, and in small towns outside of Edmonton, Alberta. During his MA, he served on the poetry editorial board of *The Fiddlehead*, and was co-founder and poetry editor of *Qwerty* magazine. Weaver's poetry has been published in numerous magazines and anthologies. Now completing his PhD at the University of Alberta, Weaver teaches first year English and is the co-founder of The Olive Reading and Zine Series.